# Can You Find It?

# Pets
## A Can-You-Find-It Book

by
Lauren Kukla and
Aruna Rangarajan

PEBBLE
a capstone imprint

# Bug Buddies

Can you find
these things?

rocket

hot dog

cowboy
boot

clock

 ant      cactus      bird      tree      penny      Dalmatian

## Pet Shop Pals

Can you find
these things?

chick

paw print

chicken

bee

 leaf

 bird

 masked bunny

 hamster

 apple

 corn

# Cozy Cats

Can you find these things?

truck

green button

coffee cup

stop sign

bead

donut

goldfish

teddy
bear

car

heart

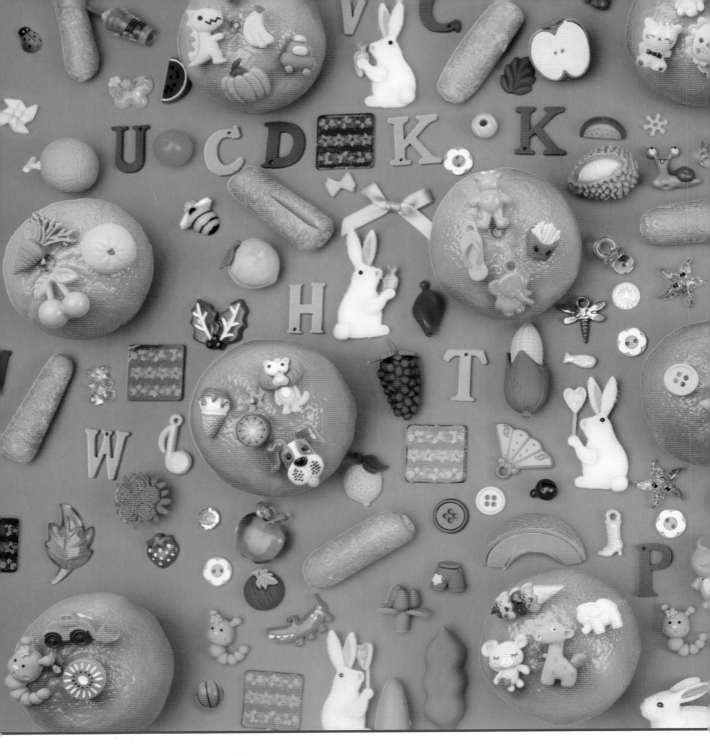

# Bunny Yummies

Can you find these things?

alligator

bee

ice cream

**S**

letter S

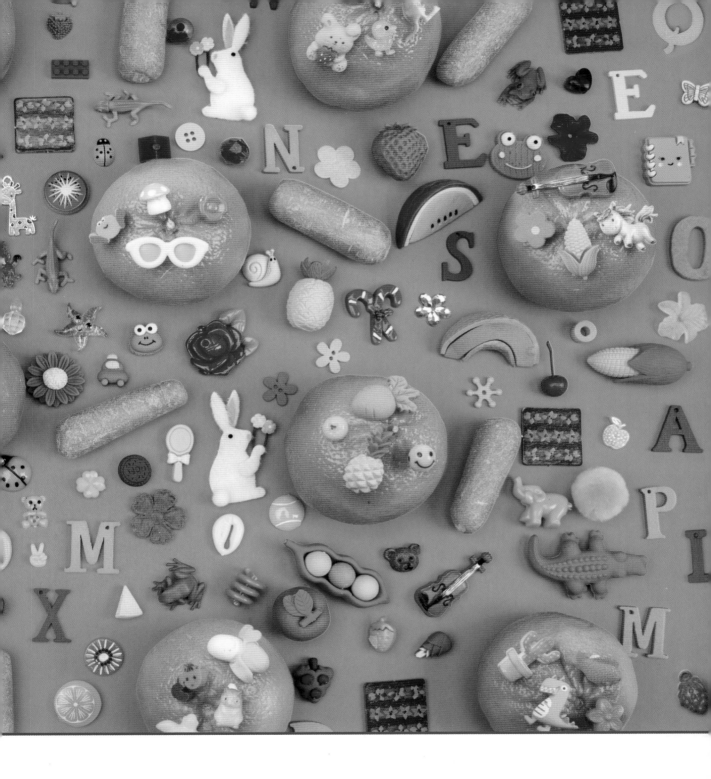

 bananas

 crab

 fish

 cactus

 green apple

 cookie

# Home Sweet Hamster

Can you find these things?

 cat

koala

 bat

 acorn

 lion

 pig

 French fries

 jam jar

 horse

 milk jug

# Turtle Time

Can you find
these things?

football

fruit slice

die

sports
car

clothespin

duckling

eye

cat

rocking
horse

monkey

# Dog Park Days

Can you find these things?

pink fire hydrant

rabbit

violin

spotted dog

 gummy
bear

 cupcake

 hamburger

 avocado

 pineapple

 tennis
ball

# Singing Birds

Can you find
these things?

dolphin

sunglasses

lollipop

bike rider

lemon

birdcage

kite

apple

purple
butterfly

triangle

# Radical Reptiles

Can you find these things?

egg and toast

hat

sea star

crown

 bunny

 pinwheel

 bulldozer

 basketball

 building brick

 kangaroo

# Fish Friends

Can you find
these things?

cloud

mirror

ghost

dragonfly

 angel

 candy

 flower

 boat

 raindrop

 elephant

# Pets in Space

Can you find these things?

dress

cheese

donut

umbrella

shoes

crown

airplane

pumpkin

butterfly

gold
shuttle

# Backyard Chickens

Can you find these things?

teacup

headphones

golden egg

waffle

 dragonfly

 peace sign

 bike

 bucket

 UFO

 watermelon

# Pocket-Sized Pets

Can you find
these things?

green
rose

jingle bell

shooting
star

teapot

 chef's hat

 popsicle

 eggplant

 cardinal

 fox

 mushroom

# Muddy Paws

Can you find
these things?

mustache

brown
puzzle piece

panda

horse

soda
bottle

umbrella

scissors

key

purple
daisy

game
controller

Psst! Did you know that a pair of blue swim shorts was hiding in EVERY PUZZLE in this book?

It's true! Go back and look!

## Look for other books in this series:

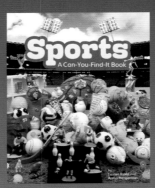
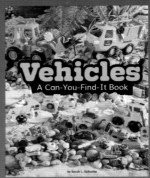

Pebble Sprout is published by Pebble, an imprint of Capstone.
1710 Roe Crest Drive, North Mankato, Minnesota 56003
capstonepub.com

Library of Congress Cataloging-in-Publication Data is available on the Library of Congress website

ISBN: 9781666397086 (hardcover)
ISBN: 9780756572754 (paperback)
ISBN: 9780756572457 (ebook PDF)

Image Credits: Scenes by Mighty Media/Lauren Kukla, Aruna Rangarajan; Shutterstock: Kay Cee Lens and Footages, cover (sky), NIPAPORN PANYACHAROEN, cover (tree), varuna, cover (fence, grass), Yaroslav Vitkovskiy, 1 (space background)

Printed and bound in China.   P05130